SMALL BATCH

Sweets

ISBN-13: 978-1-56383-567-4
Item #7144

**Printed in the USA
by G&R Publishing Co.**

Distributed By:

CQProducts

507 Industrial Street
Waverly, IA 50677

www.cqbookstore.com

gifts@cqbookstore.com

CQ Products

CQ Products

@cqproducts

@cqproducts

What's in Your Pantry?

When to keep an item, when to toss it out, or how to bring it back to life:

Baking Chocolate ... If yours has a white film on it, it's still safe to use and the flavor won't be affected.

Baking Powder ... Stir ½ tsp. into 1 C. hot water. If it foams, it's still fresh enough to use.

Baking Soda ... Add a pinch of it to 1 tsp. vinegar. If it fizzes, it's still good.

Honey ... If you find your honey has crystalized, microwave for 30 seconds or warm in a pan of simmering water.

Olive Oil ... Once it goes bad, it will smell rancid; that's your sign to pitch it.

Nuts ... Give them the sniff test. You can usually tell if they don't smell "quite right." Freeze for optimum freshness and shelf life.

Self-Rising Flour ... For best results, replace every six months.

Spices ... They don't go bad, but if they no longer smell vibrant and are past their prime, add a bit more or toss 'em and buy new.

Vanilla Beans ... Rehydrate dried out ones by submerging in warm water for 10 minutes. After that, they should be good to go.

Vinegar ... It may turn cloudy, but that's OK – it's simply an aesthetic change; the vinegar can still be used.

Whole-Grain Flour ... Do the sniff test, same as for nuts *(above)*. Freeze to keep fresh longer.

Makes 4

Peach Deep-Dish Mini Pies

1¾ C. plus 2 T. flour, divided

½ tsp. salt

½ C. coconut oil

1 tsp. orange zest

4 to 5 T. orange juice or water

3 fresh ripe peaches, peeled & diced

1 tsp. vanilla

¼ tsp. ground cardamom, divided

½ C. plus 3½ tsp. sugar, divided

1 T. butter, cut into small pieces

1 beaten egg or egg white

½ C. heavy cream

Preheat your oven to 350°. Grease four 3½" custard cups and sprinkle with sugar. In a bowl, combine 1¾ cups flour and the salt; add the oil, orange zest, and orange juice and mix with a fork until well blended. Press the dough into a log and cut into five even pieces; set one piece aside. Place each of the remaining pieces into a prepped custard cup; press the dough into the bottom and up the sides, trim, and crimp the edges.

Stir together the peaches, vanilla, ⅛ teaspoon cardamom, ½ cup sugar, and the remaining 2 tablespoons flour. Divide the fruit mixture evenly among the four crusts and top with the butter.

Roll or press the set-aside dough to ⅛" thickness and cut out four shapes with a small cookie cutter; brush with egg, sprinkle with 1½ teaspoons sugar and lay one cut-out on top of each pie. Set the pies on a rimmed baking sheet and bake 30 to 35 minutes or until the crusts are golden brown, covering with foil if the cut-outs start to brown too quickly. Remove from the oven and let stand until the filling thickens.

Beat the whipping cream with the remaining 2 teaspoons sugar and ⅛ teaspoon cardamom until stiff peaks form. Serve with the pies.

Makes 12

Waffled Snickerdoodles

To make the cookies, in a small bowl, whisk together ¼ C. softened butter, ¼ C. sugar, and 2 T. brown sugar until light and smooth; stir in 2 T. egg substitute *(or a beaten egg yolk)* and ½ tsp. vanilla. In another bowl, mix ½ C. plus 2 T. flour with ⅛ tsp. baking soda, ⅛ tsp. cream of tartar, ½ tsp. cinnamon, and ⅛ tsp. salt; add to the butter mixture and stir well. Preheat a waffle iron to medium-high heat and spritz with cooking spray. Using a level tablespoon of dough for each cookie, place four evenly spaced mounds of dough on the hot iron. Close and cook until browned, 1 to 2 minutes. Carefully remove the cookies to a cooling rack and repeat with the remaining dough.

For the glaze, whisk together 1 oz. softened cream cheese, 3 T. powdered sugar, and ½ tsp. vanilla until smooth; stir in enough milk to make a drizzling consistency. Drizzle over cookies and sprinkle with cinnamon-sugar.

Easy Java Cinnamon Rolls

Preheat your oven to 350° and spritz a 9" round cake pan with cooking spray. Unroll and separate the rolls from 1 (17.5 oz.) tube refrigerated cinnamon rolls *(with cream cheese frosting packet included)*; set aside the frosting. Arrange the rolls in the prepped pan and bake about 25 minutes or until golden brown and no longer doughy. In the meantime, put ½ C. chopped walnuts in a small rimmed baking sheet and place in the oven for 10 minutes, until toasted, then set aside.

In a small microwave-safe bowl, microwave 1 T. milk on high about 20 seconds, until hot; stir in 1 tsp. instant coffee granules, stirring until dissolved. Stir in the set-aside frosting and heat in the microwave on high for 20 seconds, until hot. Stir in ½ C. white baking chips and heat 25 seconds longer or until melted, stirring until smooth. Stir in the toasted walnuts and spread evenly over the baked rolls. Serve warm.

Serves 6

Butterscotch Pumpkin Parfaits

2 oz. cream cheese, softened
½ (15 oz.) can pumpkin puree
1 tsp. cinnamon
¼ tsp. ground allspice
3 T. plus ¼ C. brown sugar,
  divided

2 C. heavy cream, divided
1¼ C. crushed gingersnap
  cookies
Butterscotch ice cream
  topping

In a mixing bowl, beat the cream cheese, pumpkin puree, cinnamon, allspice, 3 tablespoons brown sugar, and 1 cup cream on medium speed until thick and creamy; chill until needed. Put a clean bowl and clean beaters in the freezer for 15 minutes.

In the chilled bowl with chilled beaters, whip the remaining 1 cup cream on high speed until soft peaks form. Sprinkle in the remaining ¼ cup brown sugar and beat until stiff peaks form.

In each of six 6-ounce glasses, layer cookie crumbs, the pumpkin mixture, a drizzle of butterscotch topping, and whipped cream to fill half the glass. Repeat the layers, ending with a mound of whipped cream. Drizzle on a bit of butterscotch topping and sprinkle with a few cookie crumbs.

Use some of the remaining pumpkin puree to make Pumpkin Pie Bars on page 50.

Caramel Affogato

Drizzle caramel ice cream topping in a chilled cup. Then simply add a scoop of caramel ice cream (ours was caramel swirl with chocolate-covered caramel chunks) and another drizzle of caramel topping. Pour hot espresso or strong coffee over the top. That's it!

Affo-WHAT? *Affogato is the Italian word for drown. Ice cream drowned in espresso? Yes please.*

9

Dark Chocolate Cupcakes

¼ C. plus 2 T. flour
¼ C. sugar
2 T. unsweetened cocoa
 powder
½ tsp. baking soda
¼ tsp. salt

¼ C. plus 2 T. milk at room
 temperature
2 T. grapeseed oil or olive oil
1 tsp. vanilla
Raspberry Buttercream
 (recipe below)

Preheat your oven to 350°. Line four regular muffin cups with liners, spritz with cooking spray, and set aside.

In a medium bowl, combine the flour, sugar, cocoa powder, baking soda, and salt. In a separate bowl, stir together the milk, oil, and vanilla. Add the wet mixture to the dry ingredients and stir until just incorporated *(do not over-mix)*. Divide the batter among the prepped muffin cups, set the cups on a rimmed baking sheet, and bake 22 to 25 minutes, until a toothpick comes out clean.

Remove the cupcakes from the muffin cups to cool. Frost the cooled cupcakes with Raspberry Buttercream and garnish if you'd like.

Raspberry Buttercream

In a mixing bowl, beat ½ C. softened butter on medium-high speed until light and fluffy. Beat in ½ tsp. vanilla. Gradually add 1½ C. sifted powdered sugar, beating on low speed until combined. Stir in 2½ to 3 T. seedless red raspberry preserves or spreadable fruit until incorporated. *(Red food coloring can be stirred in with the preserves if desired.)*

Makes 4

Makes 4

Apple-Cinnamon Scones

½ C. chopped pecans, divided

1 C. flour

1 tsp. baking powder

¼ tsp. salt

¼ tsp. cinnamon

⅛ tsp. baking soda

2 T. sugar

¼ C. cold butter, cut into pieces

1 egg yolk

¼ C. plus 1 T. half & half

½ C. finely chopped, peeled apple *(we used Granny Smith)*

2 T. cinnamon baking chips

½ C. powdered sugar, sifted

1 tsp. pure maple syrup

Preheat your oven to 425° and line a cookie sheet with parchment paper. Dump the pecans onto the paper and bake 8 to 12 minutes, until toasted; remove from the cookie sheet, finely chop, and set everything aside *(keep the parchment paper on the cookie sheet for later)*.

Stir together the flour, baking powder, salt, cinnamon, baking soda, and sugar. Using a pastry blender or two knives, cut the butter into the flour mixture until it resembles coarse crumbs. In a small bowl, whisk together the egg yolk and ¼ cup half & half until well blended; stir into the flour mixture until just combined. Stir in the apple, baking chips, and half the toasted pecans.

Turn the dough out onto a lightly floured work surface, working a bit of the flour into the dough if it's too sticky to handle. Form into a 6" circle, about ¾" thick and cut into four even wedges. Arrange on the prepped cookie sheet and bake 15 to 18 minutes, until golden.

Let the scones cool on the cookie sheet for a minute, then move to a wire rack to cool completely.

For the glaze, whisk together the powdered sugar, syrup, and the remaining 1 tablespoon half & half until smooth. Drizzle over the cooled scones and top with the remaining toasted pecans.

Serves 2

Bread Pudding & Caramel Sauce

Preheat your oven to 350° and grease a 16-ounce baking dish *(ours was 6½" square)*. Cut day-old cinnamon-raisin bread into ¾" cubes to measure 1½ C. and place in an even layer in the prepped dish. In a bowl, whisk together 2 eggs, 1 C. half & half, ¼ C. sugar, ¼ tsp. cinnamon, ⅛ tsp. ground nutmeg, and a pinch of salt until well blended. Pour the mixture over the bread cubes and bake 40 to 45 minutes or until a knife inserted near the center comes out clean.

To make the sauce, stir together 2 T. melted butter and ¼ C. brown sugar in a small saucepan; bring to a boil, add ¼ C. half & half, and stir until blended. Serve over warm bread pudding.

Maple Walnut Fudge

Makes 6

In a small skillet over medium-high heat, toast ⅓ C. coarsely chopped walnuts until lightly browned, shaking the skillet occasionally; set aside. Line six mini muffin cups with liners; spritz with cooking spray and brush up the edges to coat well.

In a microwave-safe bowl, combine ½ C. white baking chips, 2 T. sweetened condensed milk, and 2 tsp. butter; heat on high, stirring every 15 seconds until smooth (do not over-heat). Stir in ¾ tsp. maple flavoring until just combined, then stir in the toasted walnuts. Divide the fudge evenly among the prepped muffin cups and refrigerate 1 hour or until set.

Use some of the remaining sweetened condensed milk to make Frozen Lime Cheesecakes on page 17.

Makes 6

Frozen Lime Cheesecakes

4½ graham cracker rectangles, crushed *(about ½ sleeve)*

2 T. melted unsalted butter

2 oz. cream cheese, softened

½ C. sweetened condensed milk

3 to 3½ T. lime juice

Zest of 2 limes

1 C. whipped topping, thawed

Line six standard muffin cups with foil liners. In a small bowl, stir together the cracker crumbs and butter. Set aside.

In a big mixing bowl, beat the cream cheese on medium speed until smooth. Add the sweetened condensed milk and lime juice, beating until well combined. Fold in the lime zest and whipped topping until incorporated. Divide the mixture evenly among the prepped muffin cups and top with the cracker mixture, pressing to adhere. Freeze for 4 hours or until set.

Turn the cheesecakes upside down onto a tray and carefully peel away the foil liners. Garnish however you'd like.

Use some of the remaining sweetened condensed milk to make Maple Walnut Fudge on page 15.

Serves 3

Raspberry Tiramisu

4 oz. cream cheese, very soft
   (don't use low-fat or fat-free)

1 T. sour cream at room
   temperature *(don't use low-
   fat or fat-free)*

2 T. plus ⅔ C. heavy cream,
   divided

2 egg yolks

2½ T. sugar

½ tsp. vanilla

9 ladyfingers

¼ C. cold coffee

2 C. fresh raspberries

Unsweetened cocoa powder

Whisk together the cream cheese, sour cream, and 2 tablespoons cream until very smooth; set aside.

In the top of a double boiler, whisk together the egg yolks and sugar until pale yellow, about 2 minutes. Set over simmering water and cook on low heat, whisking constantly, until mixture thickens and forms a ribbon trail on the surface when whisk is lifted, 5 to 6 minutes. Remove from the heat to cool for 3 minutes. Whisk in vanilla and the set-aside cream cheese mixture until smooth.

In a chilled bowl with chilled beaters, beat the remaining ⅔ cup cream until stiff peaks form. Fold into the cream cheese mixture.

Generously brush the tops of the ladyfingers with coffee; cut each cookie into four pieces and place a layer of cookies in the bottom of three 8-ounce serving glasses. Top with a layer of cream cheese mixture and a layer of fresh raspberries. Repeat the layers, ending with a layer of the cream cheese mixture on top; dust with cocoa powder. Cover and chill at least 1 hour before serving.

3-Ingredient P.B. Cookies

Cream together 1 C. peanut butter (creamy or crunchy), 1 C. sugar, and 1 egg. Divide the dough into 12 balls, roll in sugar, and arrange 2" apart on a cookie sheet. Press a criss-cross pattern into each with a fork. Bake at 350° for 8 to 12 minutes, until toasty brown. **Makes 12**

Only 3 ingredients needed for a super-easy, super-fast treat!

Banana Cream Pies

¼ C. sugar

1½ T. cornstarch

⅛ tsp. salt

1¼ C. whole milk

1 egg

1 T. butter

½ tsp. vanilla

1 or 2 bananas, peeled & sliced

1 (4 oz.) pkg. graham cracker mini pie crusts *(6 ct.)*

1 C. whipped topping, thawed

For the filling, combine sugar, cornstarch, and salt in a small saucepan; whisk in the milk and egg until well mixed. Place over medium-low heat and slowly bring mixture to a boil, stirring constantly until thickened. Remove from the heat and whisk in the butter and vanilla until smooth. Let cool about 10 minutes, then place plastic wrap on the surface of the filling and refrigerate until cool.

To assemble the pies, arrange 3 or 4 banana slices in each crust. Spoon the filling into the crusts, spreading evenly to cover the bananas. Spread whipped topping over the pies and chill about an hour. To serve, top with more banana slices if you'd like.

This banana filling is creamy, mild-tasting, and oh-so-light (sort of like biting into a cloud).

21

Makes 6

Makes 6

Mocha-Doodle Baked Alaskas

Coffee or mocha ice cream
6 (3") sturdy snickerdoodle
  cookies
1 C. sugar
¼ C. water

1 T. light corn syrup
Pinch of salt
4 egg whites at room
  temperature
⅛ tsp. cream of tartar

Put one large scoop of ice cream on top of each cookie and set in the freezer to harden. Make the meringue by combining sugar, water, corn syrup, and salt in a heavy saucepan; bring to a boil over medium-high heat, stirring once or twice to dissolve sugar. Cook the syrup without stirring until a candy thermometer registers 238° to 240°. Meanwhile, beat the egg whites until foamy using a stand mixer fitted with a whisk attachment; add the cream of tartar and beat until soft peaks form.

When the syrup has reached the correct temperature, gradually pour it down the side of the mixing bowl in a slow steady stream while beating the egg whites on medium speed. When all the syrup has been added, beat on high speed until meringue forms almost-stiff peaks and is cool.

One at a time, remove a cookie/ice cream combo from the freezer. Place generous blobs of meringue over the ice cream; spread to attach to the cookie and swirl to make decorative peaks and valleys, making sure the ice cream is completely covered. Return to the freezer for at least 30 minutes. *(To store for later, wrap the assembled desserts individually and freeze for up to one month.)*

Before serving, preheat your oven to 525°. Place desserts on a broiler pan and bake about 2 minutes, until nicely browned. *(Instead of baking, these can be toasted with a culinary torch.)*

Meringue-Topped Fruit

If you have a little meringue left in the bowl after making the Baked Alaskas, spread it onto fresh berries and brown with a culinary torch.

Serves 4

Apple Dessert Nachos

Coarsely chop pretzels to measure ½ C. and break 1 Heath candy bar into smaller pieces. In a small microwave-safe bowl, heat ½ C. white baking chips with ½ tsp. shortening until melted; in a separate microwave-safe bowl, heat ¼ C. creamy peanut butter until melted. In a third bowl, microwave ¼ C. caramel sauce until warm. Core and cut 2 Granny Smith apples into ¼"-thick slices and arrange on a big plate. Drizzle half the melted white chips, half the peanut butter, and half the caramel over the apples. Sprinkle with all the pretzels and Heath bar pieces. Then drizzle with the remaining melted chips, peanut butter, and caramel. Serve immediately for best results.

Nachos never tasted so sweet!

Lemon Microwave Cake

Coat an 8- to 12-ounce microwave-safe mug with cooking spray. In a bowl, combine 3 T. flour, ¼ tsp. baking powder, and ⅛ tsp. salt. Whisk in 1 egg, 3 T. sugar, 2 T. vegetable oil, 1 tsp. lemon zest, and 1½ T. lemon juice until well blended. Transfer to the prepped mug and microwave on 50% power for 45 seconds; stir and microwave 45 seconds to 1 minute more, until the cake starts to pull away from the mug and tests done. Stir together a few tablespoons of powdered sugar with a little lemon juice to drizzle over the cake. Garnish any way you'd like.

Make an extra one for a friend!

26

Makes 2

Quick Cherry Crisps

1½ C. frozen sweet dark cherries, thawed, juice reserved

4 tsp. cornstarch

¼ tsp. almond flavoring

⅛ tsp. ground ginger

¼ tsp. plus ⅛ tsp. cinnamon, divided

2 T. flour

2 T. quick oats

2 T. brown sugar

2 T. melted coconut oil or canola oil

Cut the cherries in half and put them with their juice into a medium bowl. Stir in the cornstarch, almond flavoring, ginger, and ¼ teaspoon cinnamon. Divide the mixture among two small microwave-safe bowls.

In a small bowl, mix the flour, oats, brown sugar, and the remaining ⅛ tsp. cinnamon. Add the oil and combine with a fork. Sprinkle half the mixture over each bowl of cherry filling.

Microwave on high 3 to 5 minutes or until the filling is bubbling around the edges. Let stand a few minutes to thicken before serving, or chill first. *(Instead of microwaving them, these crisps can be baked in a 350° oven for 25 to 30 minutes.)*

Makes 1

Mini Banana Bread Single

Preheat your oven to 350° and grease a 3 x 5″ mini loaf pan with butter; set aside. Mash 1 small ripe banana in a medium bowl. Add 3 T. softened unsalted butter, 3 T. sugar, and 2 T. honey; stir well. Add 1 egg yolk and stir until well blended. Sprinkle in ½ C. flour, 1 T. wheat germ, ¼ tsp. plus ⅛ tsp. baking soda, and a pinch of salt; stir to incorporate. Gently stir in 1 T. each mini semi-sweet chocolate chips, chopped maraschino cherries, and finely chopped walnuts. Pour into prepped pan and bake about 35 minutes, until a toothpick comes out clean. Cool slightly in the pan before removing to a cooling rack to cool completely.

To make a glaze, mix ¼ C. powdered sugar, ¼ tsp. each vanilla and cherry flavoring, and enough milk to make a drizzling consistency. Drizzle over cooled bread, then slice.

Serves 2

Frozen Hot Cocoa

Place two 12-ounce glasses in the freezer to chill. In a medium microwave-safe bowl, microwave 3 oz. chopped semi-sweet baking chocolate with 1 T. milk on high until melted, stirring occasionally. Stir in 2 tsp. powdered hot cocoa mix until dissolved. Add ¼ C. powdered sugar and slowly whisk in ½ C. milk until very well blended; set aside to cool.

Pour the cooled chocolate mixture into a blender and add 1 C. milk and 3 C. ice cubes. Cover and process until thick. Pour into the chilled glasses and top with whipped cream, shaved chocolate, tiny marshmallow bits *(such as Kraft Mallow Bits)*, and peppermint candy if you'd like.

Serves 6

Retro Broken Glass Dessert

½ C. pineapple juice

½ (.25 oz.) envelope unflavored gelatin *(1¼ tsp.)*

1 C. graham cracker crumbs

¼ C. melted butter

3 T. brown sugar

4 (3.5 oz.) gelatin dessert cups *(we used lime and orange flavors)*

¾ C. heavy cream

3 T. sugar

½ tsp. vanilla

Generously spritz a 5 x 9" loaf pan with cooking spray and set aside.

Microwave the pineapple juice in a glass measuring cup for 40 seconds, until hot but not boiling. Stir in the unflavored gelatin until dissolved. Refrigerate the mixture until cool and thickened, 20 to 30 minutes, stirring occasionally.

Meanwhile, make the crust. In a small bowl, stir together the graham cracker crumbs, butter, and brown sugar. Press crumb mixture into the prepped pan and set aside.

Cut the gelatin desserts into small cubes with a sharp knife and dump the pieces into a medium bowl, separating them; set aside.

In a chilled bowl with chilled beaters, beat the cream on medium speed until foamy; gradually beat in the sugar and vanilla until almost-stiff peaks form. Add the whipped cream and chilled juice mixture to the bowl of gelatin cubes and gently fold everything together until cubes are evenly coated. Spoon the mixture over the crust and refrigerate until set, at least 3 hours.

To serve, run a warm knife around the edge of the pan to loosen the dessert and then slice as desired.

Gelatin dessert cup 4-packs can be found easily in grocery stores. Search out convenience stores which often sell the cups individually.

Strawberry-Pretzel Parfaits

2 C. mini pretzels
¼ C. melted unsalted butter
¼ C. sugar
2¼ C. sliced fresh
   strawberries

4 oz. cream cheese,
   softened
¼ C. brown sugar
½ C. whipped topping,
   thawed

Toss the pretzels into a food processor. Add the butter and pulse until incorporated and the pretzels are coarsely chopped. Transfer the mixture to a medium skillet and toast over medium heat 8 to 10 minutes, stirring often. Dump the pretzels on some paper towels and set aside to cool.

Stir together the sugar and strawberries and set aside for 30 minutes.

In a small bowl, stir together the cream cheese and brown sugar until smooth; measure out ¼ cup, mix with the whipped topping, and set aside.

Layer the remaining cream cheese mixture, pretzel mixture, and strawberries evenly among four 6-ounce dessert glasses. Top with the set-aside whipped cream mixture. Garnish if you'd like.

Makes 4

Serves 6

Salted Rolo Skillet Cookie

¼ C. softened butter
¼ C. sugar
¼ C. brown sugar
1 egg yolk
½ tsp. vanilla

¾ C. flour
¼ tsp. salt
¼ tsp. baking soda
½ C. mini Rolo candies
Chocolate syrup

Preheat your oven to 350° and grease an 8" oven-safe skillet.

In a mixing bowl, beat together the butter, sugar, and brown sugar on medium speed until combined. Add the egg yolk and vanilla and beat until smooth.

In a separate bowl, stir together the flour, salt, and baking soda. Gradually beat the dry ingredients into the butter mixture on low speed until just incorporated. Stir in the mini Rolos and press the dough evenly into the prepped skillet. Bake 15 to 20 minutes or until the edges are beginning to brown.

Cut into wedges and drizzle with chocolate syrup.

Replace the Rolos with another candy (try mini Peanut Butter Cups, M&Ms, chopped Snickers, or other favorites).

P.B. Krispies Single

Butter a 14-ounce wide mouth, microwave-safe mug and add 2 tsp. butter, 2 T. peanut butter, and ¾ C. mini marshmallows. Microwave on high 20 to 30 seconds; stir until smooth. Stir in 1 C. Rice Krispies and press into the mug. If you'd like, top with warm peanut butter, chocolate syrup, and/ or chocolate frosting. Dig in with a spoon or let it set up first – if you're patient enough.
Makes 1

Makes 2

Half-Pint Blueberry Cobblers

Mix 1 T. sugar with ½ tsp. lemon zest and set aside. Microwave 1½ tsp. butter in each of two half-pint mason jars until melted. Brush the butter around to coat the inside of the jars; sprinkle a little sugar all around the insides.

In a bowl, stir together ¼ C. sugar, ½ C. flour, ¾ tsp. baking powder, and ¼ tsp. salt; whisk in ⅓ C. milk. Divide the batter evenly among the jars. In a clean bowl, lightly mash 1 C. fresh blueberries and stir in 1 tsp. of the set-aside lemon-sugar. Divide the berries over the batter and sprinkle with the remaining lemon-sugar. Cover with paper towels and microwave on high 2 to 3 minutes, checking every 30 seconds until done. Garnish if you'd like.

Makes 2

Crème Brûlée for Two

Preheat your oven to 325°. Whisk together 3 egg yolks, ½ C. heavy cream, ¼ C. sugar, and the seeds from 1 vanilla bean; toss in the vanilla bean pod and let stand for 15 minutes. Discard the bean pod and divide the egg mixture evenly among two shallow ramekins. Set the ramekins into a rimmed baking dish, set on the middle oven rack, and fill the dish with enough hot water to reach halfway up the sides of the ramekins. Bake 30 to 40 minutes, until set but slightly jiggly in the center. Remove the ramekins from the baking dish, let stand 15 minutes, then refrigerate uncovered for 2 hours. Remove the desserts from the refrigerator and set at room temperature for 30 minutes before serving.

When you're ready to serve, sprinkle on a nice even coating of sugar to cover the top, then toast with a culinary torch until browned. Top with fruit if you'd like (we topped ours with sugar-coated peach slices and lightly browned them with the torch).

Makes 6

Itty Bitty Peanut Butter Pies

1½ C. milk, divided
3 T. sugar
2 T. cornstarch
Pinch of salt
2 egg yolks, beaten
7 T. creamy peanut butter

Mini semi-sweet
  chocolate chips
1 (4 oz.) pkg. graham cracker
  mini pie crusts *(6 ct.)*
Whipped topping, thawed
Chopped roasted peanuts

Set aside 2½ tablespoons of the milk and pour the remainder in a medium saucepan; heat over medium heat until hot but not boiling.

In a medium bowl, stir together the sugar, cornstarch, and salt. Whisk in the egg yolks and the set-aside milk. Whisk half the hot milk into the egg yolk mixture until smooth and then gradually whisk the egg mixture into the milk remaining in the saucepan. Cook over medium heat a few minutes, until the mixture boils and thickens, whisking constantly. Remove the pan from the heat and whisk in the peanut butter until melted.

Put a single layer of chocolate chips in the bottom of each crust, and pour the warm filling evenly over the chips. Serve warm or place plastic wrap on the surface of the filling and refrigerate until cool.

Serve topped with whipped topping and a sprinkling of peanuts and chocolate chips.

Try this

Mini graham cracker crusts are great to keep on hand for use with all kinds of fillings. Try a smore's-inspired treat by filling with ice cream, then adding some marshmallow crème and chocolate sauce.

Makes 4

Waffle Iron Brownies

3 oz. bittersweet baking
  chocolate, chopped
¼ C. butter
½ tsp. instant coffee crystals
1 tsp. hot water
1 egg
½ C. sugar

1½ tsp. unsweetened
  cocoa powder
½ tsp. vanilla
¼ tsp. salt
1 C. flour
Optional toppings

In a microwave-safe bowl, combine the chocolate and butter; microwave in 30-second intervals, stirring until melted and smooth. In a separate bowl, dissolve the coffee crystals in the hot water. Set both aside to cool slightly.

In a medium bowl, whisk together the egg, sugar, cocoa powder, vanilla, and salt. Stir in the coffee and chocolate mixture until well blended. Add the flour and stir until just combined.

Preheat a Belgium waffle iron on medium heat and coat with cooking spray. Place four evenly spaced mounds of batter on the hot iron. Close and cook 1 to 2 minutes, until lightly browned and done. Turn off the iron, open the lid, and leave brownies in place for 1 or 2 minutes.

Carefully remove each brownie and transfer to a wire rack to cool. Top with frosting, caramel or chocolate sauce, whipped topping, fruit, and/or ice cream if you'd like.

Serves 6

Pear & Almond Skillet Cake

½ tsp. baking powder
¼ tsp. baking soda
½ tsp. coarse salt
1 tsp. cinnamon
1 C. flour
¼ C. softened unsalted butter
½ tsp. vanilla

¾ C. plus 1 T. sugar, divided
1 egg
Zest of ½ orange
½ C. buttermilk
2 ripe pears, peeled, each cut into 12 slices
1 to 2 T. sliced almonds

Preheat your oven to 375°. Butter the bottom and sides of an 8" cast iron skillet and dust lightly with flour; shake out excess.

Stir together the baking powder, baking soda, salt, cinnamon, and flour. In a mixing bowl, beat butter, vanilla, and ¾ cup sugar on medium speed until pale and well combined, then beat in the egg and orange zest. Add the flour mixture alternately with the buttermilk, beating after each addition until combined.

Spread ⅓ of the batter in the prepped skillet and layer with half the pears, fanning them out. Spread the remaining batter over the pears, then fan out the rest of the pears on top. Sprinkle with almonds and the remaining 1 tablespoon sugar.

Bake 40 to 45 minutes, until golden brown and a toothpick comes out clean, covering with foil if the cake begins browning too quickly. Transfer to a cooling rack to cool slightly before slicing.

Edible Cookie Dough

*Mix 2 T. softened butter and ½ C. brown sugar until creamy. Add ⅛ tsp. vanilla, 1½ T. milk, ⅓ C. flour, and a pinch of salt; stir until well combined. Fold in a handful of mini M&Ms or chocolate chips if you'd like. Eat with a spoon or roll into tiny balls, freeze, and stir into ice cream. **Serves 1***

Keep dough in a lidded jar in the fridge and dip into it anytime you feel the urge.

Lemon-Raspberry Crêpes

½ C. flour
1 egg
¼ C. water
¼ C. milk
⅛ tsp. salt
1 T. melted butter

½ to ¾ C. lemon curd
About 2 C. whipped topping, thawed
2 C. fresh raspberries
2 T. seedless red raspberry preserves or spreadable fruit

In a medium bowl, whisk together the flour, egg, water, milk, salt, and butter until very smooth *(batter will be thin)*. Heat an 8" to 9" nonstick skillet or sauté pan over medium-high heat. Pour ¼ cup batter into the heated pan and swirl to make a thin even circle. Cook 1 to 2 minutes on each side, until lightly browned. Remove from the skillet to a cookie sheet or waxed paper to cool. Repeat to make three more crepes.

Spread 2 to 3 tablespoons lemon curd over one side of each crepe; spread a layer of whipped topping over the curd and add some raspberries. Fold or roll crepes as desired to enclose the filling. Warm up the preserves in the microwave and drizzle over the filled crepes. Garnish any way you choose.

Makes 4

Makes 3

Jumbo Carrot Cake Muffins

¼ tsp. salt
1 tsp. cinnamon
¼ tsp. ground nutmeg
Pinch of ground cloves
1½ tsp. baking powder
¾ C. flour
¼ C. whole wheat flour
¼ C. applesauce

1½ tsp. vegetable oil
¼ C. sugar
¼ C. brown sugar
1 egg
1 tsp. vanilla
¾ C. finely shredded carrots
Zest of 1 orange, divided
Cream cheese frosting,
    optional

Preheat your oven to 350° and line three jumbo muffin cups with liners. In a small bowl, stir together the salt, cinnamon, nutmeg, cloves, baking powder, and both kinds of flour; set everything aside.

In a mixing bowl, beat together the applesauce, oil, sugar, and brown sugar on medium speed until well combined. Beat in the egg, vanilla, carrots, and half the orange zest, setting aside the remainder for the frosting if using. Mix in the dry ingredients until just blended.

Divide the batter evenly among the prepped muffin cups and bake 28 to 30 minutes or until a toothpick comes out with just a few moist crumbs. Cool the muffins in the cups for several minutes before removing to a cooling rack to cool completely.

Stir the set-aside zest into the frosting and spread over the muffins if you'd like.

Mexican Churro Popcorn

Mix ⅓ C. powdered sugar, 3 T. sugar, 1 to 1½ T. cinnamon, ½ tsp. ground allspice, and ¼ tsp. salt; set aside. Dump 9 C. popped popcorn into a big bowl. Melt 3 (2 oz.) squares white almond bark in the microwave following package directions, stirring until smooth; pour over the popcorn and stir to coat. Sprinkle with sugar mixture and toss well. Serve immediately or let cool and store in an airtight container. **Serves 4**

Makes 3

Oreo Lava Cakes

5 Oreo cookies, divided
2 (3.25 oz.) vanilla pudding cups
1 C. semi-sweet chocolate chips

¾ C. milk
½ C. flour
1 tsp. baking powder
2 T. vegetable oil
Powdered sugar

Preheat your oven to 350°. Spritz three 8-ounce ramekins with cooking spray and coat with flour; shake out excess. Chop two of the Oreos into a small bowl and stir in the pudding. Chop the remaining Oreos and set aside.

In a medium microwave-safe bowl, heat chocolate chips and milk together for 1 minute; whisk until mostly melted. Microwave again for 1 minute, then whisk until smooth and well combined. Whisk in the flour, baking powder, and oil. Pour some of the batter into the prepped ramekins, filling ⅓ to ½ full. Put 2 to 3 tablespoons of the pudding mixture in the center of each ramekin and pour the remaining batter over the pudding to cover. Set the ramekins on a rimmed baking sheet and bake 17 to 18 minutes, until the surface of the cakes is just set.

Run a knife around the sides of the cakes to loosen. Place a serving plate on top of each ramekin and very quickly invert each plate and ramekin so the cake falls onto the plate. Sprinkle with powdered sugar and the remaining chopped Oreos. Serve immediately for best results.

Serves 4-6

Pumpkin Pie Bars

½ C. flour
3 T. cold butter
2 T. sugar, divided
¼ tsp. salt, divided
1¼ tsp. cinnamon, divided
½ C. pumpkin puree
1 egg

⅓ C. brown sugar
⅛ tsp. ground cloves
½ tsp. vanilla
¼ C. milk
½ C. heavy cream
⅛ tsp. ground nutmeg

Preheat your oven to 350°. Line a 5x9" loaf pan with parchment paper, letting the paper hang over the ends; spritz with cooking spray and set aside.

In a food processor, combine the flour, butter, 1 tablespoon sugar, ⅛ teaspoon salt, and ¼ teaspoon cinnamon. Pulse until the mixture is sand-like and then press firmly into the bottom of the prepped pan. Bake 15 to 18 minutes, until lightly browned.

Meanwhile, in a big bowl, whisk together the pumpkin puree, egg, brown sugar, cloves, vanilla, milk, ½ teaspoon cinnamon, and the remaining ⅛ teaspoon salt until smooth. Pour immediately over the hot crust. Bake about 20 minutes more, until the filling is set and does not jiggle when the pan is gently shaken.

Let cool completely, then refrigerate until cold. Lift out of the pan using the parchment paper and cut as desired.

To make spiced whipped cream, in a chilled bowl with chilled beaters, beat the cream until soft peaks form. Add the nutmeg and the remaining 1 tablespoon sugar and ½ teaspoon cinnamon, beating until stiff peaks form.

Use some of the remaining pumpkin puree to make Butterscotch Pumpkin Parfaits on page 8.

Homemade Chocolate Pudding

1½ T. cornstarch
1 C. whole milk
½ C. milk chocolate or semi-sweet chocolate chips

6 plain chocolate wafer cookies
8 Andes mints
Mint Whip *(recipe below)*

In a medium microwave-safe bowl, combine the cornstarch and milk, whisking until smooth. Add the chocolate chips and microwave on high for 3 to 4 minutes or until thickened and bubbly, stirring every minute. Let cool about 5 minutes, then place plastic wrap directly on the surface of the pudding and refrigerate until chilled.

When the pudding has chilled, coarsely chop the cookies and put half into each of two dessert dishes, reserving a few crumbs for the top. Spoon the pudding over the cookie crumbs. Coarsely chop the mints and sprinkle over the pudding. Add a dollop of Mint Whip and sprinkle on the reserved crumbs.

Mint Whip

Put ¾ C. thawed whipped topping into a bowl and stir in ¼ tsp. peppermint extract. For a little pop of color, you can also stir in a bit of green food coloring.

Serves 2

Serves 4-6

Apple Berry Pie

1¼ C. flour
4½ T. sugar, divided
½ tsp. salt, divided
½ C. plus 1 T. cold butter
2 to 3 T. cold water
1 T. cornstarch
¾ tsp. cinnamon
¾ tsp. ground nutmeg

3 baking apples *(we used Golden Delicious)*, peeled & thinly sliced
1 C. frozen mixed berries, thawed *(we used a strawberry/blueberry mix)*
1 egg white, beaten
1 tsp. cinnamon-sugar

To make the crust, combine the flour, 1½ tablespoons sugar, and ¼ teaspoon salt in a food processor. Slice ½ cup butter and add to the machine; pulse together until coarse crumbs form. With the machine running, slowly add water and process until dough comes together. Wrap dough in plastic wrap and chill about an hour.

Meanwhile, prepare the filling. In a medium bowl, whisk together the cornstarch, cinnamon, nutmeg, and the remaining 3 tablespoons sugar and ¼ teaspoon salt. Add the apples and toss to coat; set aside. In an 8" ovenproof skillet over medium heat, melt the remaining 1 tablespoon butter. Stir in the berries and cook for 4 minutes, stirring frequently. Stir in the set-aside apples and cook 2 minutes more, then remove from the heat.

Preheat your oven to 400°. On a floured surface, pat or roll out the chilled dough into a circle at least 1" larger than skillet; set the dough over the fruit filling, fold the edges under, and crimp. Cut slits in the crust; brush the entire surface with egg white and sprinkle with cinnamon-sugar. Bake 25 to 30 minutes or until the crust is golden brown and the fruit is bubbly.

Twinkie Shortcakes

For each shortcake, slice a Twinkie in half lengthwise. Put some sweetened sliced strawberries over the bottom half, place the top half over the berries, and add a dollop of thawed whipped topping.
Makes 1

This is a great shortcut recipe for the easiest shortcakes you'll ever make!

Serves 3-6

Blondish Brownies

Preheat your oven to 350° and grease a 4 x 6" baking dish *(adjust baking time slightly if your baking dish is a different size)*.

In a medium bowl, stir together 2 T. melted butter and ½ C. brown sugar until well combined. Stir in 1 egg yolk and 1 tsp. vanilla. Then add ⅓ C. flour, ¼ tsp. baking powder, and ⅛ tsp. salt and mix until well blended. Mix in 3 T. each butterscotch chips, your favorite chocolate chips, and sweetened flaked coconut until incorporated. Spread evenly in the prepped dish and bake about 28 minutes, until set in the middle and deep golden brown around edges. Let cool. Serve with a scoop of ice cream and drizzle with chocolate and/or caramel sauce.

Makes 6

Baby Pecan Monkeys

Preheat your oven to 350°. Coat six regular muffin cups with cooking spray. In a bowl, stir together ¼ C. melted butter and ¼ C. brown sugar and divide the mixture among the muffin cups. Sprinkle each with 1 tsp. chopped pecans. Mix 2 T. sugar and 1 tsp. cinnamon in a big zippered plastic bag. Unroll 1 (7.5 oz.) tube refrigerator biscuits, cut each biscuit into six even wedges, and toss them into the bag; zip closed and shake until completely coated. Place ten wedges into each muffin cup and bake for 15 minutes or until golden brown. Cool for a minute, then turn upside down to release.

"Monkey around" a little with this recipe by eliminating the nuts or drizzling the baked breads with warmed cream cheese frosting and/or fruit jam.

Makes 4

Chocolate-Peanut Butter Parfaits

½ C. semi-sweet chocolate chips

¼ C. milk

3 oz. cream cheese, softened, divided

¼ C. creamy peanut butter

2¼ C. whipped topping, thawed, divided

3 T. sugar, divided

1 tsp. vanilla, divided

Pinch of sea salt

1 to 1½ C. crumbled peanut butter cookies

In a small microwave-safe bowl, microwave the chocolate chips with 1 tablespoon milk on high until melted, stirring occasionally until smooth. Whisk in the remaining milk and set aside to cool slightly.

In a medium bowl, beat 2 ounces cream cheese until smooth, then beat in the peanut butter. Whisk in ¾ cup whipped topping, 2 tablespoons sugar, ½ teaspoon vanilla, and sea salt until combined.

In a big bowl, whisk the remaining 1 ounce cream cheese until smooth, then whisk in the remaining 1½ cups whipped topping, 1 tablespoon sugar, and ½ teaspoon vanilla. Fold in the set-aside chocolate mixture.

In four 8-ounce dessert glasses, make layers of cookie crumbs, the chocolate mixture, and the peanut butter mixture, ending with a sprinkle of crumbs.

This chocolate-peanut butter combo is one of the best cures for an intense craving.

for Small Batch Cookies

1 C. sugar
1 C. brown sugar
3 C. flour

1 tsp. baking soda
½ tsp. baking powder
½ tsp. salt

Stir all the ingredients together until well combined and store in an airtight container at room temperature for up to three months. Use a portion of the mix to make the recipes that follow. **Makes five cups of mix to store away to make five small batches of cookies later on.**

Chocolate Chip Cookies

Preheat your oven to 375° and line a cookie sheet with parchment paper. In a mixing bowl, beat 3 T. softened butter and ½ tsp. vanilla on medium speed until creamy. Add 1 C. prepared cookie mix and 1 egg yolk; beat on medium speed for 2 to 3 minutes, until small even crumbs form. Add 1 tsp. water and beat just until dough comes together. Stir in ½ C. semi-sweet chocolate chips, working with your hands as needed. Drop by heaping tablespoon onto the prepped cookie sheet. Bake 8 to 10 minutes, until edges are lightly browned. Cool on pan for 5 minutes, then transfer to a cooling rack. **Makes 10**

White Chocolate-Cranberry-Macadamia Cookies

Preheat your oven to 375° and line a cookie sheet with parchment paper. In a mixing bowl, beat 3 T. softened butter and ½ tsp. almond extract on medium speed until creamy. Add 1 C. prepared cookie mix and 1 egg yolk; beat on medium speed for 2 to 3 minutes, until small even crumbs form. Add 1 tsp. water and beat just until dough comes together. Stir in 3 T. white baking chips, 3 T. chopped macadamia nuts, and 2 T. dried sweetened cranberries. Drop by heaping tablespoon onto the prepped cookie sheet. Bake 8 to 10 minutes, until edges are lightly browned. Cool on pan for 5 minutes, then transfer to a cooling rack. **Makes 10**

BIG BATCH MIX

for Small Batch Bars

¾ C. softened butter
1½ tsp. salt

1 tsp. baking powder
3 C. flour

In a medium bowl, beat together butter, salt, and baking powder on medium speed until combined. Add flour and beat until fine crumbs form. Store in an airtight container in the refrigerator for up to four weeks. Use a portion of the mix to make the recipes that follow. **Makes four cups mix to store away to make four small batches of bars later on.**

Toffee Bars

Preheat the oven to 350° and grease a 5 x 9" loaf pan. In a small mixing bowl, combine 1 C. prepared bar mix, ½ C. brown sugar, 2 T. softened butter, 2 T. egg substitute *(or 1 egg yolk)*, and ½ tsp. vanilla. Beat on medium speed until smooth. Spread dough in the prepped pan and bake about 20 minutes, until top springs back when lightly touched. Immediately sprinkle with ½ C. milk chocolate chips; let stand 2 to 3 minutes to melt. Spread the chocolate over the bars and sprinkle with 2 T. chopped pecans. Cool before cutting. **Makes 6**

Oatmeal Carmelitas

Preheat the oven to 375° and grease a 5 x 9" loaf pan. In a medium bowl, combine 1 C. prepared bar mix, ½ C. quick oats, 2 T. sugar, 2 T. brown sugar, 1 tsp. vanilla, and 1 egg yolk; mix on medium speed until crumbly and well blended. Press 1⅓ C. of the mixture into the bottom of the prepped pan. Bake 8 to 10 minutes, until lightly browned around edges. Meanwhile, mix together ½ C. caramel topping and 2 T. flour. Remove the crust from the oven and sprinkle with ½ C. semi-sweet chocolate chips. Drizzle with caramel mixture, then sprinkle the remaining crumb mixture on top. Bake 17 to 20 minutes more, until golden brown. Cool before cutting. **Makes 6**

Index